ANFERNEE HARDAWAY

★

GRANT HILL

Also by East End Publishing, Ltd.

BASKETBALL SUPERSTARS ALBUM 1996
MICHAEL JORDAN * MAGIC JOHNSON
SHAQUILLE O'NEAL * LARRY JOHNSON
STEVE YOUNG * JERRY RICE
TROY AIKMAN * STEVE YOUNG
KEN GRIFFEY JR. * FRANK THOMAS
BARRY BONDS * ROBERTO ALOMAR
MARIO LEMIEUX
THE WORLD SERIES: THE GREAT CONTESTS
THE COMPLETE SUPER BOWL STORY GAMES I-XXVIII
MICHAEL JORDAN
SHAQUILLE O'NEAL
WAYNE GRETZKY

For more information on how to order these books, as well as many other exciting sports books, see the back pages of this book.

ANFERNEE HARDAWAY

★

GRANT HILL

BRIAN CAZENEUVE

EAST END PUBLISHING, LTD.
SYOSSET, NY

To Anne Cazeneuve, whose love and encouragement can never be appreciated enough, and to the memory of Arturo Cazeneuve, whose passion for words—and sports—I carry on.

*ANFERNEE HARDAWAY * GRANT HILL*
First Printing / September 1995
ISBN 0-943403-35-9

The cover photo of Anfernee Hardaway was supplied by SPORTSCHROME EAST / WEST. The photo of Grant Hill was taken by Tim O'Dell. Cover design by Jim Wasserman.

Copyright © 1995 by Richard J. Brenner/East End Publishing, Ltd.

Library Systems and Services Cataloging in Publication Data

Cazeneuve, Brian.
    Anfernee Hardway * Grant Hill / Brian Cazeneuve.
        p.   cm.

    ISBN 0-943403-35-0

    1. Hardway, Anfernee. 2. Hill, Grant. 3. Basketball players—United States—Biography. I. Title.

GVSS4.H24C39 1995   796.323´092 B--dc20

Provided in cooperation with Unique Books, Inc.

This book is published by East End Publishing, Ltd., 54 Alexander Drive, Syosset, NY 11791.

For information regarding author visits to student groups, contact East End Publishing, Ltd., 54 Alexander Drive, Syosset, NY 11791, (516) 364-6383.

Contents

ANFERNEE HARDAWAY

1. Two Names—No Frills

On July 18, 1971, Anfernee Deon Hardaway was born into conditions that would test his will to make a better life for himself. Anfernee grew up in a poverty-ridden section of Memphis, Tennessee, where many children often got in fights, attended poor schools and lived in families with at least one parent away from home.

The children who grew up in Anfernee's neighborhood and went on to live productive lives did so by beating the odds. They often had a little bit of luck, they usually had a little bit of love, and they always discovered that the one essential ticket to success was hard work. Those children were the fortunate ones.

Anfernee got his unusual name because his mother, Fae Patterson, had a friend with the same name. Fae liked the name because it was so unusual, and so she chose it for her son.

But by the time Anfernee was old enough to recognize his own name, most people knew him as Penny. His grandmother, Louise Hardaway, started calling the boy "pretty," but a family friend thought she was saying "Penny." The misunderstood nickname stuck, and the child with the unusual first name was then known to his friends as Penny.

The boy's father, Eddie Golden, left the family when Penny was a baby and only came back to see to his son on rare occasions. When Penny was in first grade, his mother, a singer by trade, was having trouble finding work in the economically depressed area. She was also worried about the frequent shootings and stabbings in the neighborhood. For a while, Fae took Penny to her mother's bigger house in a slightly safer section of town. She found a few odd jobs, but finally decided that it would be best to leave Penny with his grandmother while she looked for work elsewhere. Fae eventually went to California, where a friend helped her find some steady work as a lounge singer.

Penny's mom didn't come back to Memphis to live with him until he was about to enter high school.

In the meantime, six-year-old Penny stayed in Memphis with his grandmother, a cook in the city's school system. The walls in their house had cracks everywhere and roaches found their way in and out of the holes. Still, living there was better than what his mother could give him at the time, and so he was able to look toward a better life.

"It was hard and confusing at first, because I thought nobody really wanted me," Penny recalls. "But my grandmother proved that she loved me and cared about what happened to me. All the love from all the fans in the world wouldn't have meant anything without the love of my grandmother."

Penny's sense of abandonment stayed with him for years. He was always looking for approval from people, for a chance to belong. He was usually very quiet in elementary school and somewhat unsure of himself. Other kids picked on him from time to time because he was tall and skinny and looked awkward when he walked. Sometimes Penny was so concerned about the way he walked that he would find a reason to stop in the hallway when a teacher, a buddy or a cute girl walked past him in the other direction.

He gradually discovered that the place where he belonged was on a basketball court, even if it was just a playground near his school where there were no nets on the crooked rims. The older kids, who didn't accept him on the court when he was eight years old, were eager to have 11-year-old Penny join their games once he could keep up with them.

At his grandmother's urging, Penny stayed away from drugs as he got older, even though some of his friends were also friends of drug dealers who, in effect, ruled the neighborhood. It was hard going home every day looking over his shoulder and wondering if somebody was going to jump out from behind a building and attack him for his spare change. When that happened a few times, Penny usually got away but one time he wound up with a split lip after trying to defend himself.

Penny felt lucky when he made it to Memphis's Treadwell High School. He knew that he had a focus that could give him a sense of belonging. That focus was basketball.

2. All Play—No Work

Penny's skills were so strong that he became an instant starter at Treadwell. His coach, Garmer Currie, immediately inserted Penny into the starting lineup as the team's point guard, and he took over the reins as the team's floor general. After having solid, but not star-studded, seasons as a ninth- and tenth-grader, Penny really began to shine in his junior year.

People began calling him "Magic" because of the obvious comparisons to Magic Johnson, the Lakers' legendary point guard. Like Magic, Penny was becoming known for the versatility in his game. At 6-feet-5-inches and still growing, he was tall for a point guard and, as Magic did at 6-feet-9-inches, he could post up smaller guards inside and shoot over them with ease. Like Magic, he was also extremely quick, with great court awareness and exquisite ability to lead a fast break. Like Magic, Penny was an excellent rebounder. His all-around skills, added to a great leaping ability and determined work ethic, helped make him a stingy defender, who would usually lead his team in both steals and blocks. There was also a style to Penny's game: the no-look passes, the high-flying dunks that made people think his game was downright magical.

In his final two seasons at Treadwell, Penny became the first player in history to win back-to-back High-School-Player-of-the-Year honors for the State of Tennessee. He was also named *Parade Magazine's* National High School Player of the Year during an outstanding senior-year season in which he averaged 36.3 points, 10.1 rebounds, 6.6 assists, 3.3 steals and 2.8 blocks per game.

Penny's outstanding play raised many eyebrows among college coaches. But being from Memphis and wanting to stay close to home, Penny liked Memphis State, which has since changed its name to the University of Memphis. He already knew a lot about the head coach, Larry Finch, whose nephew, David Vaughn, was a friend of Penny's and was also headed to MSU in the fall to play for his uncle. Penny was nervous about going to college, but felt comfortable about becoming a Memphis State Tiger after talking with Finch.

"It's a different world playing in front of 20,000 people instead of 500," the coach said of Penny's decision. "With that many folks, it helps when he feels he's really at home."

But before Penny could wield his courtside magic at MSU, he first had to straighten himself out in the classroom. After skipping a number of classes in his senior year at Treadwell and flunking algebra for most of the year, Penny failed to reach the minimum scores on his college entrance exams that were necessary for him to participate in NCAA-sanctioned sports as a freshman. Penny could attend classes at Memphis State, but according to the NCAA's Proposition 48 rule, he couldn't play basketball there until his scores improved.

"I was lazy in high school," Penny admitted. "I didn't think grades were important. Sometime people just gave me grades because I was a good basketball player. They didn't make me study. They weren't helping me at all. But then, I wasn't helping myself, either."

Penny had a long talk with his mother and grandmother who told him that he had a great opportunity in front of him, a chance most kids in his neighborhood would never get. But it was up to him to do the schoolwork.

Penny had to earn 24 college credits, a little less than the average number of credits for a college year, before the Prop 48 guidelines would allow him to participate in sports at MSU. In his first semester, he earned 17 credits and maintained a B-average in his classes. In the spring, he earned 15 more credits and upped his average to a B. He didn't have to sign up for summer classes, but he took two courses and received nine more credits with a B in both classes. Penny had lived up to his end of the bargain, fulfilling the promise he had made to his mother and grandmother by passing all of his courses. Although he had missed a year of eligibility, Penny had made the most of his second chance and made himself eligible to play basketball at Memphis State in his sophomore year.

3. Shots

Despite his academic turnaround, Penny was still prone to occasional poor judgment. Late in the spring semester of his freshman season, Penny survived a frightening experience that would forever change his life. He had been out late one night in the Memphis suburb of Binghamton with a friend of his named Terry Starks, when the two decided to walk to the house of Penny's cousin, LaMarcus Golden. Penny had known that Terry often ran with a rough crowd and had probably done some things he shouldn't have. But Penny still considered Terry a friend and chose to overlook the potential dangers of hanging out with the wrong crowd.

As Penny and Terry waited outside the house, three men drove alongside them in a car. One of the three stopped to ask directions, and as Penny stopped to help him, another man got out of the car, pulled out a pistol and told Penny and Terry to lie face down on the ground. While they were lying down, Penny and Terry had their money swiped from their pockets by the third man, who also robbed them of the basketball sneakers they were wearing. One of the muggers referred to Terry by name several times, even though Terry told Penny later that he didn't recognize any of them.

As the men drove off, Penny started to get up, apparently too fast for one of the robbers, who fired three shots in Penny's direction. The first two shots missed his head by several feet, but the third one ricocheted off the sidewalk and lodged in his right foot.

Penny tried to stay calm and wait for the police and an ambulance to arrive. He knew then that he shouldn't have been hanging out with Terry, given Terry's shady past. He was scared that he might never get to play basketball if his foot didn't heal properly.

Penny was rushed to The Regional Medical Center in Memphis, where doctors decided not to remove the bullet, which was lodged in such a way that removing it might have caused nerve damage. Instead, the doctors placed the foot in a cast and told Penny he would have to wait for the soft tissue to grow around the affected area before they could take the bullet out.

For three months, Penny underwent therapy to take care of his foot before doctors were finally able to remove the bullet. The incident also gave him time to think about what had happened and about his future.

"I was studying harder, but I wasn't worried about what was going on around me," Penny recalled. "I'm glad it happened the way it did, because I could've gotten killed. Then my mother would've had to hear that somebody shot her son, that he never made it. That whole scene straightened me out. It scared me. Now I won't take anything for granted."

4. Time to Play

By December, Penny's foot had healed and he was ready for action. But after a year-long wait he was very nervous before his first collegiate game in the Pyramid, MSU's new arena. He was so jittery before the contest against DePaul, in fact, that he thought he would throw up during the pregame shootaround. That shaky feeling carried over into the game, as Penny scored just three first-half points on 1-of-8 shooting.

"I went into shell-shock in the first half," he said later. "I wasn't letting the game come to me. Then I settled down a little."

Penny stepped up his pace in the second half and wound up scoring 18 points, including a clutch three-pointer in the closing seconds, to send the game into overtime. He also hauled down 15 rebounds, dished out 6 assists, blocked 4 shots and made 4 key second-half steals. But Penny also missed all three of his free-throw attempts and committed 13 of Memphis State's school-record 31 turnovers. Some of the miscues were typical of Penny's tendency to try to do too much. On consecutive possessions during the overtime, for example, he tried to force the ball inside with a pair of bullet passes, while a lot of time remained on the shot clock. One pass was intercepted; the other one was deflected out of bounds by one of his teammates, and both turnovers led to DePaul baskets. The costly miscues were the main ingredients in the Tigers' 92–89 loss.

Afterwards, Coach Finch talked to his team about knowing when to be patient and when to be aggressive. Penny realized that many of these comments were directed at him, since he was the Tigers' floor general. Still, Penny felt confident that he had gotten some of the nervous excitement out of his system with his first college game and that better times lay ahead.

Before the opening tip of the Tigers' second game against Murray State, Finch tapped Penny on the shoulder and instructed him to "take care of the ball." Penny got the message and toned down his game. Instead of reaching for the spectacular, he opted for safe passes and waited for the right chances to penetrate. True, Penny scored just 11 points in 35 minutes and went 0-for-4 from downtown. But he also turned the ball over only twice in the entire game. The Tigers reduced their turnover total to 11, and rolled to an easy 78–54 victory.

While Penny did rein in his game to some degree, he still retained the ability to make dramatic plays. He just made better decisions about when to unleash his arsenal. In a game against nationally ranked Tulane, Penny hit an off-balance three-pointer with four seconds left to put the Tigers in front, 68–67. Then on the next play, he stole Tulane's inbound pass and successfully dodged defenders who tried to foul him before the clock ran out, sealing Memphis State's victory.

"We got beat by a great shot from a great player," Tulane's coach Perry Clark said after the game. "You don't see many like him."

Penny's schoolyard skills also came to the fore in a game against Southwest Louisiana. Penny had driven to the basket and was hoping for a foul call after falling hard to the floor near the opposing basket. The officials let the play go, as the Tigers scrambled to get back on defense without Penny. After a missed shot, Memphis State's Tony Madlock grabbed the rebound and heaved the ball towards Penny, who had run up to midcourt. The ball sailed over Penny's head and bounced just in front of the foul line. Penny, though, followed the flight of the ball, waited for it to come down, set himself, and, in one motion, cupped the ball in his right hand and dunked it through the basket. Even the crowd at Southwest Louisiana couldn't help but give him a standing ovation.

"Hardaway is the only player in college basketball I'd actually pay to see play," ESPN analyst Dick Vitale said after the game. "He is awesome. He can score, dish and clean the glass.

Hardaway is Mr. Versatility." And he was only part of the way through his first season of college ball.

Penny was literally doing it all. He gained confidence throughout the season in running the team's offense, and on numerous occasions he narrowly missed triple-doubles, games in which players break into double digits in three statistical categories—usually points, assists and rebounds. In an overtime victory against St. Louis, Penny even flirted with a quadruple-double, recording 17 points, 10 rebounds, 8 assists and 7 steals.

Having sprouted to 6-feet-7-inches, he had a rare combination of size and quickness that made him difficult to defend because most guards were too small and most forwards were too slow to cover the fleet-footed backcourt man.

Defensively, Penny was equally comfortable in Coach Finch's man-to-man and zone defenses. He was the Greater Midwestern Conference leader, from Game 1 through the end of the season, in the combination of blocks, which are usually made by centers and power forwards, and steals, which are usually made by guards.

He not only played well, he also played with flair, and he helped his team win. In a six-week stretch late in the season, Penny was named the Conference Player of the Week three times. His dunks were the subject of ESPN's Plays of the Week twice, and the Tigers won 10 of 12 games to vault them to a 20–10 record and a berth in the 1993 NCAA tournament. What's more, Penny had conquered his opening-game skittishness. After committing 13 turnovers against DePaul, Penny never turned the ball over more than seven times in any subsequent contest.

5. Tournament Time

With 21 points and 8 rebounds, Penny led the Tigers to an opening-round victory against Pepperdine. In the second round, MSU drew the nationally ranked Arkansas Razorbacks, and the deck appeared to be stacked against the Tigers. Penny picked up three quick fouls, and wasn't his usual aggressive self. As a result, the Tigers fell behind 44–36 at half-time, and trailed by 12 early in the second half.

It was then that the Hardaway-David Vaughn combination went to work. In one sequence of four possessions, the pair combined to lead the Tigers on a 9–0 run: First, Penny fed David for a fast-break dunk; on the next time down, David took a pass from Penny, drew a double-team and passed back above the top of the key, where Penny drained a three-pointer; Penny then forced the Razorbacks into a turnover and gave Vaughn a lead pass that led to a foul and two free throws. The Dynamic Duo capped off the run when Vaughn grabbed a rebound and instead of shooting, passed to Penny, who faked a jump shot, dribbled around his man along the baseline, and tossed in a soft bank shot over a smaller defender.

The sequence showed off all of Penny's skills: his ability to shoot, run the floor, pass and play defense.

"If you can find a first-year player with a more polished game than Hardaway, show him to me," Arkansas coach Nolan Richardson said, adding in what may have been an exaggeration, "I want him on my team. If you take Larry Bird, Magic Johnson and Michael Jordan and roll them all into one player, that's the way I see Anfernee Hardaway."

The game, though, was still in doubt in the final minute, when Penny picked up his fifth foul and had to leave the floor. With the score tied at 80–80, Vaughn knocked down the game-winning shot with five seconds to play, as the Tigers nipped the

Razorbacks, 82–80.

The Tigers then traveled to Kansas City, where they were a considerable underdog to Georgia Tech, a team that had gone to the Final Four the previous season. The Tigers, though, rallied from a three-point deficit in O.T. and managed to tame the Yellow Jackets, 83–79.

Penny finished with team-high figures of 24 points, including five three-pointers, and seven assists, while committing only one turnover all afternoon.

In the regional final, the Tigers again had to face the Cincinnati Bearcats, a team that had beaten them three times during the regular season. In each game, Penny was matched against Nick Van Exel, the Bearcats' lightning-quick sharpshooting guard who now plays for the Los Angeles Lakers. Van Exel had given Penny trouble each time the teams met, and this game was no exception.

It took Penny just 12 minutes to pick up his third foul, a close call made with a late whistle, on a play in which Penny thought he had made a clean steal from Van Exel. At the time, the Tigers held a slim 23–21 lead. But after Penny went to the bench, the Bearcats began to take control of the game, rolling to a 46–36 half-time lead.

This time, the Tigers' task was tough to tackle. The Bearcats finished with a flourish, demolishing Memphis State 88–57. Penny, who eventually fouled out, finished as his team's leading scorer with just 12 points.

After the game, Finch praised his team for its work ethic, reminding the players that it was sweat and determination that had brought the Tigers to their first final-eight appearance since 1985. He wanted to give the players something to build on, while at the same time reminding them to work even harder during the off-season, since, as he told them, "Now that people know you can play, you will be the hunted next year instead of the hunter."

6. Magical Comparisons

Penny had worked hard on the court and in the classroom. In the spring semester of the 1991-92 academic year, Penny took five classes—biology, American history, algebra and two education classes—instead of the typical four classes, and recorded a 3.2 grade-point average (out of a possible 4.0) for the term, the highest of any player on the team.

On the court, Penny was named MVP of the Greater Midwest Conference and was chosen as an AP All-American. He led the team in scoring average (17.4), assists (5.5) and steals (2.4), and set a school record for three-pointers in a season (69). Penny proved just what a complete player he was by being the only player in Division 1-A to rank in the top five in his conference in points, rebounds, assists, steals and blocks.

But Penny wasn't going to sit back and admire his accomplishments. He also worked on his jump shot. He routinely drove to the MSU field house, where he took about 350 shots a day from all angles on the floor. It was during one such workout that he learned he had been one of the college stars invited to practice and play scrimmage games against the Dream Team, the incredible assemblage of the NBA's most talented stars who would represent the United States in the 1992 Olympic Games later that summer.

Although the scrimmages were designed to give the Dream Team a chance to get used to playing together before their pre-Olympic qualifying tournament in Portland, the games were surprisingly competitive. In one scrimmage, a 30-minute game, Penny spent a lot of time guarding Magic Johnson, the player people said he most resembled. Although Magic outscored Penny 10 to 8 in the game won by the Dream Team, 77–73, Penny made a deep impression on the Magic Man.

"It was like looking in the mirror and playing against myself," said Magic. "So many guys have been compared to me and they all flop. But Anfernee is the first guy who really is like me. My game is up in my head, and his is, too."

Later that summer, after the U.S. team won the gold medal in Barcelona, Penny was honored when Magic asked him to organize a Magic-Penny charity game in Memphis. The proceeds benefited several charities in the local area, including college scholarship programs, as well as drug and AIDS-awareness programs and clinics. Since the game itself was for a good cause, most of the players tried to entertain the crowd and played very little attention to defense. Penny did his part by scoring 29 points, adding 16 assists which helped his team overcome a 27-point half-time deficit. But Magic poured in 49 points and recorded a triple-double to help his team hold on for the 160–158 victory.

7. Walking the Rocky Road

Despite the loss of six graduating seniors—but only one starter—the Tigers were considered a legitimate threat to reach the Final Four, especially since the Hardaway-Vaughn combination had another year of experience to draw upon. Preseason polls had the Tigers ranked anywhere from No. 3 to No. 11. But in the team's season-opener against Arkansas, the Tigers suffered a tremendous blow when Vaughn suffered a torn ligament in his knee and was lost to the team for the season. With Vaughn grounded, Penny knew that he would face more double-teaming and have to assume a greater burden of the MSU offense.

For a while Penny didn't handle the pressure well. He struggled through the Tigers' second game of the season against in-state rival Tennessee, missing four straight late-game shots, while MSU lost its lead and then the game, 70–59. The loss marked the first time since 1975 that the Tigers had started the season 0–2. Despite the bad start and Penny's struggles, he still did enough to be named conference Player of the Week. But he began to feel that a potentially great season was going to waste.

"All summer I thought it would be our year," he recalled. "Then David went down, and it's like we lost our hunger, like we thought, 'We can't be at full strength, so what's the point?' "

Things got worse before they got better, as the Tigers dropped a heartbreaking home-opener to Tulane, 86–85, for their third loss in a row. After the game, Penny did what a lot of 20-year-olds do when things aren't going well—he called his mother. He told her he was starting to feel the pressure of the team's poor start. More important, he worried about *her*, about how much he wanted to buy her a bigger house in a safer environment. Fae knew that Anfernee was sincere, but she also told him that this was something they could talk about after the season. For now, she told him, think about playing well in the next game and studying hard for the next big test at school.

The talk reinforced a constant theme in Penny's life: Work hard, but don't become so overwhelmed that you try to do much at once. The talk also energized Penny, which, in turn, helped the slumping Tigers. The team finally bounced back with three straight victories. And on the day before the Tigers headed to Maui for a tournament in Hawaii, Penny received an A on a test and an A- on a paper. The turn of events relaxed him, and allowed him to look forward to seeing Hawaii for the first time.

In Maui, Penny played some of the best basketball of his college career. In the first game of the four-team tourney, he poured in a career-high 37 points, including six treys, although Memphis State dropped the game to BYU in overtime. The next night Penny led the Tigers past Louisiana State 70–66, making a highlight-film block late in the game to preserve the win.

Penny even got to enjoy a little of Hawaii. The Tigers went on a team cruise around the island, and the players spotted a rare humpback whale, an especially large whale with a curved back and long flippers. Penny called his mother to try to explain the sight of such an unusual animal. He was more upbeat this time as he talked with her about his future. He thought about the ways in which basketball was helping him see a world that could be so different than the one he had grown up in. In many ways he felt more fortunate than he had at any time in his life, yet he still thought of home and he still thought about entering the NBA draft so he could sign a pro contract and have the money to share some of his opportunities with his mother. Again she told him to wait until after the season before talking to her about it in detail.

Unfortunately, the joy of 80-degree December days in Hawaii was short-lived. The Tigers traveled north to Minnesota, where they were met with a snowstorm and subzero temperatures. To make matters worse, three starters were nursing injuries and the team was as cold as the weather. Penny poured in 30

25

points, but the Tigers lost to the University of Minnesota, 70–55.

After the game, Coach Finch called the players into his hotel room and gave them a tongue-lashing.

"You guys are feeling sorry for yourselves," he told them. "You're looking at the injuries we have and you're making excuses for yourselves. You spend your whole lives fighting through adversity to get the chance you have at this university, and then you play like this."

The coach's words were intended for the whole team, but nobody took them to heart more than Penny. Even though his recent play had been superb, he still felt he could raise his game to another level.

Prior to the team's next homestand, no Tiger had ever recorded a triple-double. But over a dazzling three-game stretch, Penny *averaged* a triple-double. His numbers: 27.3 points, 14.0 rebounds and 10.0 assists. Both *The Associated Press* and *Sports Illustrated* named him their Player of the Week, and ESPN named him the Athlete of the Week, an award given to the best performer of the week, regardless of what sport he or she plays.

Thanks largely to Penny, after the team's poor showing in Minnesota, MSU went 12–2 over the course of its next 14 games and closed the regular season with a 19–10 record. Although the Tigers suffered a second-round loss in the Greater Midwest Conference tourney, their strong finish earned them another berth in the NCAA tournament.

Just as pleasing to Penny and his mother and his grandmother was his strong showing in the classroom during the first semester. For the second straight term, Penny won the team prize for having the highest marks on the club. He was majoring in education, minoring in business, and thinking of becoming a teacher or a counselor someday.

8. Moving On

The unranked Tigers drew the 20th-ranked Western Kentucky Hilltoppers as their first-round tournament foe in Orlando, Florida. Both major newspapers there ran huge stories about Penny on the front pages of their sports sections on the day before the game, and several of the Hilltoppers mentioned that they felt the public had given them short shrift in talking about the game.

The Tigers opened with a flourish, rolling to a 13–6 lead before the first time-out. Then things started to fall apart. Memphis State didn't make a field goal until Penny's lay-up seven minutes later. Despite the fact that they shot just 20% over the last 15 minutes of the half, the Tigers used their scrappy defense to keep them ahead 28–24 at half-time.

In the second half, the teams see-sawed back and forth. With just 2:39 to play, Western Kentucky built its largest lead, at 51–46, but the Tigers clawed their way back into a 51–51 tie with less than a minute to play. Then Penny sank a three-pointer that appeared to give the Tigers the lead with 46 seconds left. But an official had spotted MSU's Billy Smith standing in the lane for too long, and whistled him for a three-second violation, nullifying what would have been the go-ahead basket.

In the final half-minute, the Hilltoppers sank four free throws and the Tigers managed just one foul shot in their last two possessions, leaving Memphis State on the short end of a 55–52 score.

Despite the disappointment in the NCAA tournament, the MSU athletic department was making a strong pitch for Penny to win National Player of the Year honors. The publicity effort was spearheaded by Mark Owens, the basketball team's sports information director. Owens helped design an 11-inch copper penny with a depiction of Anfernee in action on one side, a profile of him on the other, with a list of his achievements lightly scrolled across both sides. In a matter of hours, the SID office was swamped with orders to buy the pennies, or, as the office called them, "Pennys."

Penny wound up finishing second in most Player of the Year votings to Indiana's Calbert Chaney, but he did win the Greater Midwest Conference Player of the Year award for the second straight season and had cumulative averages of 22.8 points, 8.5 rebounds and 6.4 assists per game over his two seasons at MSU.

As soon as the season ended, the big question around the MSU campus was whether Penny was going to return for his senior season or enter the NBA draft. He didn't have an answer for them, only more questions for himself. Penny had a right to be proud of the way he had bounced back academically. He wanted to graduate with his class and to give MSU an extra year because of the opportunity the school had given him. But he also wanted to help his mother and grandmother, especially when he thought of their bare-minimum lifestyle. He knew that if he left school a year early and made himself eligible for the NBA draft, the team that picked him would offer him a contract that would allow him to give his mother some of the things the family never had, such as a chance to live in a safe, clean neighborhood.

Finally, on the eve of April Fools' Day, Penny decided that he would leave school and apply for the draft. Penny, though, left MSU in a blaze of glory, doing so well on his final exams that he earned a spot on the dean's list, a mark of academic excellence.

Shortly after the semester ended, Penny had a chance to work with the Orlando Magic's All-Star center, Shaquille O'Neal, who was filming a basketball movie in Frankfort, Indiana called *Blue Chips*. The film starred Nick Nolte as the college basketball coach of a fictional school, Western University. Many real-life basketball players appeared in the movie, including Anfernee, who played Shaq's teammate, and, in a number of the basketball scenes, fed him perfect alley-oop passes as part of the film script.

"I knew from watching him on the set that this was a guy I wanted to play with in the NBA," Shaq recalled. "He played with a lot of confidence, even when we were just fooling around. Sometimes you can just tell which guys will be able to click together in game situations. I can't explain it, but we had a chemistry. We had this one scene where the director told us we might need a lot of takes. Penny was supposed to throw an alley-oop. First take, voomp. Right there. Slam. Cut. Thank you. Print it. Next scene."

9. A Magical Draft

Penny had hit it off with Shaq while filming *Blue Chips* and wanted to play for the Magic, but it was almost certain that Orlando, which owned the first pick in the NBA draft, would use it to draft Michigan's strong forward, Chris Webber. Penny figured he would go to the Philadelphia 76ers at No. 2, the Golden State Warriors, who had the No. 3 pick, or the Dallas Mavericks, who would pick fourth. After Webber, several scouts speculated, Penny would be among a group of three potential picks including Shawn Bradley, the 7-feet-6-inch center who had taken the previous two years off from Brigham Young University in order to do missionary work overseas, and Jamal Mashburn, Kentucky's high-scoring 6-feet-8-inch forward.

It was routine practice for NBA teams to ask prospective draft picks to work out for them and take physical exams. Penny had done this for many teams, including the Magic, who watched him work out a second time on the day before the draft. Penny's second workout was a smash. He hit shots from every angle, scored high on quickness and reflex drills, and figured he had made a positive impression on the Magic officials. He was absolutely correct.

"I've never seen someone do the things that Penny Hardaway did in that workout, making passes and dunks that would have had a crowd screaming in disbelief," said Pat Williams, the Magic's general manager.

At first it looked as though Penny was right. The Magic selected Webber with the first pick. The Sixers took Bradley next and then the Warriors chose Penny. Reporters were still interviewing the Hardaway family about Penny's move to the West Coast, when he learned that the Warriors had just traded him and three future first-round draft choices to Orlando for Webber.

The swap caught the Orlando faithful off-guard. Fans

watching on a big-screen TV in Orlando cheered when they heard that the Magic had picked Webber, drooling at the thought of an athletic strong forward teaming up with Shaq in an awesomely powerful front court.

When the trade for Penny was announced, the cheers quickly turned to loud booing. Around the league, however, knowledgeable people were saying that the Shaq and Penny duo could be to the 1990s what Los Angeles Lakers stars Kareem Abdul-Jabbar and Magic Johnson were to the 1980s.

"You have the potential to have the premier point guard and the dominant center on the same team again as you did in L.A.," Magic coach Brian Hill said. "They'll only get better as they get older. They're both unselfish players.

"Every so often a player comes along who has a special label on him. Anfernee Hardaway is one of those unique players who makes other players around him better. He can score, rebound and play defense from the point guard spot. He's the master of the no-look pass. He's a lot like John Stockton in that he encourages his teammates to run the floor, because they know he'll find them. If they work to get open, he'll get them the ball," added Hill, as he compared his untried rookie to the NBA's all-time assists leader.

The Magic structured a creative 13-year contract offer that would allow Penny to make $45 million guaranteed and borrow $20 million more, interest-free, over the duration of the contract. However, the deal also allowed him to renegotiate the contract one time after a year in which he achieved certain statistical goals. That meant that Penny's deal would keep the Magics under the salary cap, but it also meant that the two sides might have to rework another deal as early as 12 months later.

To Penny, the best thing about the contract was simple—he could finally buy his mother and grandmother a nice house. Penny was overjoyed at being able to give something back to his family.

Even Shaq, who had signed for less money the previous year, said he didn't resent Penny's contract. Of course Shaq was also making even more money from endorsements than he was from his basketball salary, thanks to sizable contracts with Reebok, Pepsi and Spalding, among others.

Shoe companies also wanted Penny to endorse their product. It was a strange sense of power that players of his stature often had. A nod of approval from a Shaq or a Penny or a Michael Jordan could mean a new line of sneakers costing $100 or more for a single pair. At first, Converse called with a take-it-or-leave-it offer to make Penny their No. 1 celebrity endorser. Penny advised his representatives to wait to hear what other companies had to say. He listened to an offer from Reebok, the shoes endorsed by Shaq, but finally settled on Nike, the company represented by Jordan, Charles Barkley of the Phoenix Suns and two-sport star Deion Sanders.

Such attention was quite a change from the way Penny used to think of sneakers. "All these years I've been looking at shoes I couldn't afford," he said. "Now I'm telling the company what shoes to sell."

But some fans did resent Penny's riches in light of the fact that he hadn't yet played a game and hadn't proven that he could fill the sneakers of Chris Webber. After reading some of the negative stories in the Orlando papers, Penny worried that it might take a while to win over the fans, and his concerns were well founded.

10. Winning Over the Crowd

Penny didn't do anything to help his cause when he scored just four points and committed six turnovers in the team's exhibition home-opener against the Miami Heat. The crowd, which had given him only a lukewarm reception when he entered the game, was downright hostile by the end of the night.

Ironically, one of the players who helped Penny through the difficult transition to the pros was Scott Skiles, the Magic's starting point guard the previous season, who had set the NBA single-game record with 30 assists in one game several years earlier. Penny had assumed that Skiles would give him the cold shoulder since the veteran was probably going to lose his starting job as soon as the rookie was ready to move from the two-guard position into the role as starting point guard. But instead, Scott took Penny under his wing, encouraging the youngster and reminding reporters and fans to be patient with him.

"People need to realize that the transition from the college game to the pro game is difficult," Skiles said. "I've said all along that Penny's going to be an excellent player. He can be an All-Star. He has the skills and a great attitude. As time goes on, people are going to see him blossom."

Penny's on-court confidence grew as his and his family's off-court life became more settled. He made sure his mother and grandmother moved into their new home. He also rented his own house and invited two older and responsible friends from Memphis to stay with him. The more Penny was able to assume responsibilities in his off-court life, the more confidence he began to show in fulfilling Skiles's prediction.

He was still tentative about looking for his shot, what with Shaq waiting inside for an entry pass most of the time. But almost immediately, Penny began gaining a reputation for his outstanding defense.

Many rookies have a tough time adjusting to playing defense in the NBA, where seven-footers routinely set hard picks against guards, where zone defenses are forbidden, and where defenders are not allowed to hand-check the man they are guarding until he dribbles past the opposing foul line. But Penny was on a defensive roll. In one four-game stretch, opposition players guarded by Penny averaged just seven points. Clyde Drexler, a veteran NBA all-star who scored just five points, was amazed by Penny's tough "D."

"He makes you look bad," said Drexler, the Houston Rockets' backcourt ace who was still playing for the Portland Trail Blazers at the time. "He made *me* look terrible."

Penny, on the other hand, was looking better and better. On November 23, Penny even silenced the O-Rena boo-birds, when he put on a million-dollar performance in leading the Magic to a big home-court victory against Webber and the Warriors.

Penny also helped make the Magic a much better team than the one that had finished at 41–41 the previous season. At the All-Star break, Orlando was 12 games above .500. Because of Shaq, who was among the league's scoring leaders throughout the season, Penny was generally not Orlando's first offensive option. But when he unleashed his offensive skills, Penny was a joy for fans to watch. He put on a spectacular show during the NBA's rookie game during All-Star Weekend in 1994. With his flying dunks and court-length drives, Penny scored 22 points in 22 minutes and was named MVP of the game.

Immediately after the All-Star break, Hill decided that Penny was ready to take over for Skiles as the team's starting point guard. But despite his success, Penny was still very sensitive to criticism and always worried about being accepted by the fans. He even hired a cook at his house so he wouldn't have to go out to restaurants too often and hear criticism from rude fans.

Penny seemed unaware of the fact that the fans were finally starting to take him to their hearts. At the end of the season, he was very pleasantly surprised to learn that he had won the Magic Fans' Choice Award, essentially a popularity contest among Orlando fans to choose their favorite player. And the cheers for his name during the pregame introductions at Orlando's home building, the O-Rena, were matched only by Shaq's. Despite the acclaim, Penny still couldn't get the boos from draft night entirely out of his mind.

11. A Different Season

Orlando had finished the regular season with a solid mark of 50–32, a nine-game improvement over the previous year. Their record was good enough to get them into the playoffs for the first time in the franchise's brief history. But Anfernee and his Magic teammates soon learned that all the victories they had enjoyed during the regular season wouldn't necessarily translate into post-season success. The lesson of the playoffs was one that many young teams had to learn before they could become successful.

In the first round, the Magic played a best-of-five series against the Indiana Pacers, a team that finished just three games behind them in the Eastern Conference standings.

In Game 1, the Magic blew a 17-point lead and dropped an 89–88 heartbreaker thanks to Byron Scott's three-pointer with two seconds to play in regulation.

In Game 2, the Magic rallied from a ten-point deficit on the strength of a then-NBA playoff record of 11 three-pointers, including four by Penny, who had 31 points heading into the game's final seconds. The Magic appeared to tie the game when Anfernee raced the length of floor and slammed home a breakaway dunk with five seconds to play. But the officials nullified the basket, ruling that they had blown the whistle for a 24-second shot clock violation against the Pacers. So, instead, the Magic had to start all over again by setting up a play from half-court. They inbounded the ball to Penny, who slipped at the foul line and had to throw up an off-balance shot at the buzzer. The shot bounced off the rim just as the clock expired, and the Pacers escaped with a 103–101 victory.

The series moved to Indiana for the third game, and the Magic seemed to play looser without the burden of having to please the home crowd once again. Orlando led 78–70 in the fourth quarter. But then Shaq had to sit for a stretch after picking up his fifth foul, and Indiana took advantage of Orlando's void in the middle, scoring 13 straight points and completing the sweep with a 99–86 triumph.

Penny was crushed. Sure the Magic was a young team that had a lot to learn, but now that he had spent most of the regular season overcoming the boos from the preseason, he would spend all summer hearing people ask him, "So what went wrong?"

That was a tough way to end a season in which Penny had developed into one of the league's outstanding young players. "We knew he was going to do a lot of things," Coach Hill said. "He proved from day one that he was going to be one of the premier players in the league."

Penny narrowly lost out in the Rookie of the Year voting, finishing second to Webber. But Penny was determined to get better during the off-season. He spent most of July and August in Houston, where his agent lives. There, he worked out with Kenny Smith and Sam Cassell, both guards with the Houston Rockets, who had just won their first NBA title in June. The three players would challenge each other to games of horse and would often hold one-on-one contests while the third man did commentary as he watched. Wouldn't it be great, they thought, if the Rockets and Magic could meet in the '95 finals.

12. Getting It Right

Because he had met the statistical requirements of his contract, Penny exercised his right to renegotiate his deal. He did that by holding out from the team's training camp, hoping his absence would force the Magic into giving him more favorable terms. This decision was popular neither with his teammates nor the fans. Articles in local Orlando papers suggested that he was putting himself ahead of the team at a time when the Magic needed him to run the show. One banner in the stands had the name Penny crossed out and replaced by a dollar sign. Finally, late in the exhibition season, with Penny still unsigned, Horace Grant, the Magic's veteran power forward, took him aside and firmly told him to get into camp one way or the other. Grant, who had won three straight NBA titles with the Chicago Bulls from 1991 through 1993, was the free agent whom the Magic had signed in the hope that he was the missing piece in the team's charge for a championship. The next day, a deal was struck, increasing Penny's contract to $70 million over nine years. Penny once again heard some early-season catcalls from the fans, only this time, he was better prepared to deal with them.

The Magic came flying out of the gate in the 1994-95 season, posting a 17–5 record, and beating the previous year's finalists, the Houston Rockets and New York Knicks, by 25 points apiece. In 12 of the team's 17 victories, the Magic mauled its opponent by ten points or more. Penny was a huge part of the team's surge, distributing the ball effectively to his teammates, assuming the scoring burden when he had to, and earning the NBA's Player of the Week award for the first week in December. After a 38-point, 12-rebound outburst against Golden State, Penny was asked what he thought about his stat line for the game.

"No good," he said. "Eight turnovers. Gotta slow down.

Have to be patient. That's what usually messed me up last year. I tried to do too much. Now I'm taking my time, seeing how to attack the defense."

Actually, the whole Magic team was attacking, hungry and eager to atone for its early playoff exit of the previous year. Orlando entered the All-Star break with the league's best record and both Penny and Shaq were voted in as starters on the Eastern Conference All-Star squad.

Penny was also gaining national exposure off the court in a series of Nike television ads. In one, he fielded a sequence of rapid-fire questions while being interviewed at a radio station. In another, Phoenix's Charles Barkley poked fun at his nickname. And in a third, Penny stood in a darkened playground and talked about how hard work had gotten him to where he was.

It was that same hard work ethic and a ton of talent that enabled the Magic to clinch its first division title late in the season. Just as Penny was growing as a player, the Magic was quickly sprouting as one of the league's elite teams. Still, the signs were mixed heading into the playoffs.

The Magic had posted the best mark in the east, 57–25, finishing with a fabulous 39–2 on their home court, 29–0 against Eastern Conference opponents. Orlando also posted the league's second-best record, trailing only the San Antonio Spurs, who had topped the NBA with a 62–20 mark. But the dark spot in the Magic's brightest season was the fact that the team had stumbled to the finish line by losing its last seven road games. And lurking in the shadows of many people's minds was Indiana's three-game sweep of Orlando in the 1994 playoffs.

The Magic's opening-round playoff opponent was the Boston Celtics, the only team that had entered 1995 postseason play with a losing record. Although Boston put up a surprisingly tough fight in the best-of-five series, the Magic closed out the Celtics' season with a 95–92 win. That game was also a curtain closer for the fabled Boston Garden, the arena in which former Celtic teams had enjoyed 16 championship seasons.

"This is history," agreed Penny, about performing in the last game ever played on the famous parquet floor. "Someday I'll tell my grandchildren I was part of basketball's past. Right now, though, we're part of the future."

The immediate future for Penny and the Magic was the Chicago Bulls and their incomparable superstar Michael Jordan, who had made a late-season return to the NBA following an 18-month retirement. Jordan's return to the team that he had led to three straight NBA titles just prior to leaving the game had made Chicago an instant championship contender.

The Magic, though, managed to overcome the Jordan mystique and to literally steal Game 1 right out of his hands. Jordan, however, bounced right back and seared the Magic for 38 points while leading the Bulls to a ten-point win in Game 2.

The scene shifted to Chicago for Game 3, but it was the same old act for His Airness, who continued to soar while scorching the Magic for 40 points. Late in the game, though, Penny made two key defensive plays that blunted the Bulls' charge and helped pave the way to a 110–101 Orlando victory.

The teams split the next two games, giving Orlando a 3–2 edge in the best-of-seven series. The Bulls, though, were threatening to set up a decisive seventh-game showdown by building a 102–94 lead with only 3:24 left in Game 6. But then the Bulls' offense went into cold storage, while the Magic was scoring the final 14 points of the game, including a nothing-but-net three-pointer by Penny.

Afterwards, Jordan was very gracious in accepting blame for the Bulls' collapse, when in reality he had carried a mediocre team farther than they could have hoped to go. He was also very respectful to the young Turks from Orlando, saying that they were good enough, despite the team's youthful make-up, to take a run at the 1995 NBA title.

Before it could take that giant step, the Magic would have

to power past the Indiana Pacers, the team that had swept them out of the 1994 playoff picture. The memory of that painfully early departure was enough to prime the Magic to want to blow away the Pacers in the 1995 Eastern Conference Finals.

But Orlando's determination turned into tightness early in Game 1, and the Magic found itself looking up at a 20–3 deficit in the opening quarter at the O-Rena. The team showed that it had real poise, though, by pulling itself out of that deep hole and defeating the Indiana Pacers, 105–101. The Magic also took the next game, as Shaq slammed for 39 points, while Penny dished out a game-high 15 assists.

After that second win, Horace Grant decided that his Orlando teammates had the right stuff. "These guys are fast learners," said Grant, whose three championship rings gave weight to his words. "They don't believe in 'Wait your turn.'"

The Pacers, though, showed their pride by rising up on their home court to win Game 3, 103–100, before tying the series with a classic nail-biter in Game 4.

Magic guard Brian Shaw thought he had turned the tide, when he nailed a three-pointer that gave Orlando a 90–89 lead with 13.3 seconds left in the fourth quarter. However, Pacer sharpshooter Reggie Miller put down a trey of his own to give Indiana a 92–90 left with 5.2 ticks left on the clock. Then Penny stepped up and drained a third straight shot from downtown that gave Orlando a 93–92 advantage with only 1.3 seconds to play.

"I thought that was the last one," admitted Penny. "I said to myself, 'No way they can top that.'"

The Pacers, though, fired the final salvo, an off-balance 15-footer by center Rik Smits that swished the nets as the game-ending buzzer sounded. "That was the most awesome display of unconscious shooting I've ever seen in my life," said Indiana coach Larry Brown. "Unbelievable."

The Magic eeked out a 108–106 home-court win to take the

pivotal fifth game before being blown out 123–96 and returning home for a decisive seventh game.

As Penny and Shaq sat together on the return flight to Orlando, they talked about the empty feeling they had after being swept by Indiana the previous spring. That emotion had stayed with both players all summer, and both remarked that they didn't want to spend the upcoming summer hearing how the Magic, for all its talent, had underachieved.

With the game still in doubt at half-time, Penny spearheaded a defensive masterpiece against the Pacers in the third quarter. Penny was everywhere, knocking passes away from Mark Jackson, the Pacers' point guard, and Miller on the outside, and darting back into the paint to force Smits into a shot-clock violation.

On the offensive end, the Magic scored on eight straight possessions to build their lead to 25 points and rolled to a 105–81 series clinching win.

13. Rocket Launchings

The Rockets, sparked by the MVP play of center Hakeem Olajuwon, had won the 1994 NBA championship. The 1995 squad also featured Clyde Drexler, the perennial All-Star guard who had been obtained in a midseason trade with the Trail Blazers.

Throughout the playoffs, the Rockets, who, at 47–35, finished with only the sixth-best mark in the West, defeated teams with stronger winning records. Having stunned the Utah Jazz, Phoenix Suns and San Antonio Spurs, the Rockets were trying to become the first team in NBA history to win four series without home-court advantage on their way to a title. The Rockets had many heroes in their previous three playoff victories, but no one was more important than Olajuwon, especially in the Western Conference finals when he thoroughly outplayed David Robinson, the 1994-95 MVP winner.

Everything was going well for in Game 1 for the Magic, who led by as many as 20 points in the first half at the O-Rena. But Smith, who scored only three first-half points, caught fire in the second half, draining his seventh three-pointer with 1.6 seconds to play in the fourth quarter to tie the game. While the Rockets were surging, the Magic was coming apart. Orlando's Nick Anderson, a 70% foul-shooter during the regular season, missed four key free-throws in the final seconds. Then, with the game tied in overtime, 118–118, Drexler put up a shot with two seconds to play. The shot missed, but Hakeem gave the rebound a backhand slap and knocked the ball into the basket for the game-winner at the buzzer.

Penny led Orlando with 26 points, but was stunned after the game. "You can't let chances like this get away," he said. "This was a bad loss." All around the dressing room, the Magic players looked completely disheartened by the setback.

It was clear from the start of Game 2 that the disappointment hadn't worn off. The Rockets thumped the Magic 117–106, despite 33 points from Shaq and 32 by Penny. This time, Cassell, a nonfactor in Game 1, came off the bench to provide the spark, scoring 31 points to go with Hakeem's 34. The Houston guards had driven the Magic crazy on their home floor, leaving Penny to assume the blame. "It's my fault," he insisted. "The blame starts here. I take responsibility."

Penny's remarks were the noble words of an emerging team leader, since he had not been the one to miss key foul shots in the first game, and had contributed strongly in Game 2. Nevertheless, in two games against Houston at the O-Rena, the Magic had lost as many home games as it had in 41 regular-season games.

The change of scenery to Houston for Game 3 didn't help. The Rockets were clicking on all cylinders, mainly because Hakeem, more smooth and graceful than a seven-footer should have a right to be, was playing the finest basketball of his life. Every time Penny or one of the other Magic guards tried to double-team him to cut down his maneuverability and keep Shaq out of foul trouble, Hakeem found an open Rocket teammate ready to drain a three-pointer.

For much of the third game, the Magic tried to let Shaq handle Hakeem on his own. The strategy helped Orlando slow down Houston's outside game and succeeded in producing a see-saw contest for most of the night. The Magic trailed 101–100 with a minute to play when Houston again worked its inside-outside game to perfection. With Penny caught in no-man's land trying to double-team Hakeem, the center passed the ball outside to Robert Horry, who sank a 25-footer that gave the Rockets a four-point lead. Penny tried to answer with his own trey on Orlando's next possession, but he fired an airball and the Rockets held on for a 106–103 victory. "It's becoming a mental thing with us," said Penny. "They're playing with confidence and it's obvious we aren't."

The Magic did its best to avoid a sweep in Game 4, staying close and leading 78–77 early in the fourth quarter. But the Rockets went on an 11–2 run and pulled away to a 113–101 victory. Hakeem was sensational, scoring 35 points, hauling down 15 rebounds and being named the Finals MVP for the second straight year.

After the game, the Magic players huddled and put their hands together as a show of togetherness for what they'd accomplished during the year and what they felt lay ahead. "This is just the start," Shaq told people. "We'll be back and we'll be better."

The lesson was one Penny had already taken to heart. In good times and bad, there was always something better to hope for and to work toward. As a boy, he had looked around his Memphis neighborhood and never stopped thinking of how he could do something better for his mother and grandmother. As a student, he looked at his mistakes in high school and worked hard to correct them and reach the dean's list in college. Now as an NBA player, he was about to be honored as a First Team All-Star, joining Utah's Karl Malone and John Stockton, San Antonio's David Robinson, and Chicago's Scottie Pippen. It was a fabulous honor for a player who had only two NBA seasons under his belt. But Anfernee Hardaway wasn't treating his NBA success any differently than he had when things in his life didn't look so rosy. "Life is a challenge. We have to learn from this," Penny told a reporter after the Magic's final game.

"After something like this, do you just have to take some time off and get away from basketball?" the man wanted to know.

"Can't get away now," Penny said. "Gotta practice. Other guys are out there somewhere shooting threes. Naw, no time off. I have to go to work."

PHOTO SECTION

Penny puts the ball on the floor
Courtesy University of Memphis

Penny is interviewed by Al McGuire
Courtesy University of Memphis

Penny looking inside for Shaq
Photo by Vincent Manniello, SPORTSCHROME EAST/WEST

Penny about to make a long pass
Photo by Tim O'Dell

Penny taking the ball to the hoop
Photo by Vincent Manniello, SPORTSCHROME EAST/WEST

Grant goes for the jam against Iowa
Courtesy of Duke University

Grant goes over Jalen Rose
Courtesy of Duke University

Grant receiving his Men's College Basketball of the Year Award
Photo by A/P WIDE WORLD PHOTOS

Grant skies and dunks
Photo by A/P WIDE WORLD PHOTOS

Grant slams at the All-Star Game
Courtesy of Reuters/Bettmann

GRANT HILL

1. Building a Hill's Foundations

Grant Henry Hill was born on October 5, 1972 in Dallas, Texas, but he grew up in Reston, a northern Virginia suburb of Washington, D.C.

Unlike Penny Hardaway, Grant was raised in a secure and prosperous neighborhood by well-to-do, college-educated parents who were always there to make sure he was well taken care of and cared for. There were fancy cars in the garage, and a piano sat in a living room that was decorated with fine art. There were many perks to growing up as Grant Hill did, but there were also strict rules and great expectations.

Calvin, Grant's dad, had been an All-America running back at Yale University, the last player to achieve that honor while attending a school in the academically top-rated Ivy League. He had also been an NFL Pro Bowl selection in 1969, the same season that he was named the NFL's Rookie of the Year. In 1972, he became the first Dallas Cowboy to rush for 1000 yards in a season, and then sparked the Cowboys to victory in Super Bowl VII. Calvin was such a high-profile personality that he became a regular subject in the "Doonesbury" cartoon strip.

Janet, Grant's mom, had majored in mathematics at Wellesley College, where she was a suitemate of the nation's future First Lady, Hillary Rodham Clinton. After getting a master's degree in mathematics and education at the University of Chicago, Janet joined forces with Clifford Alexander, formerly Secretary of the Army, to build a successful corporate consulting firm, called Alexander & Associates. The firm deals with minority hiring for companies, including Major League Baseball.

"When you're growing up, you want to have role models," Grant says. "It was very easy for me, because the best role models I could have asked for were right in my own house. My parents stressed the importance of education, athletics and being around the right people. I didn't have to go outside my family for any of that. Everything I needed, everything I had to hear, was right at home."

But as a result of his parents' accomplishments, Grant was able to travel away from home, too, and enjoy a range of rich experiences that aren't available to the average person.

When Grant was still a youngster, his parents took him to London, where he met Kingman Brewster, who was the United States ambassador to England. Grant showed off his athletic skills right in the ambassador's office by performing an impromptu handstand. Grant also got to meet the presidents of Yale and Harvard, two of America's most respected universities. Life was so easy for Grant that he didn't even have to cross a street to get to his elementary and junior high schools, which were directly in back of the Hills' home.

Although Grant's life was comfortable, he was never spoiled. His parents always stressed values such as hard work and humility. Calvin, for example, had made more money in one year of playing football than his father, Harry, had in 25 years as a construction worker. But Calvin always acknowledged how important Harry's guidance and work ethic had been to his own success, both on the gridiron and in the classroom.

And while Grant grew up with many advantages, he still had to follow the strict rules set for him by his parents, who, like their son, grew up without brothers or sisters. Janet and Calvin didn't allow Grant to attend parties until he turned 16. They permitted no phone calls to friends during the week and only one per day on the weekend, no wandering outside the neighborhood and absolutely no missing of curfew. One night, when Grant arrived home 15 minutes late, Janet was so furious that she took his watch and shattered it against his bedroom wall. "You don't use it anyway," she told him. The next month on Grant's birthday, Janet gave him his one birthday gift—his watch, fully repaired and operational again. But there were no other gifts that year.

"Some days I called her 'Mom,'" Grant recalls. "Other days, I just called her 'the General.' We were all close, and we cared for each other in different ways. Her way was to lay down the law. But she's the glue that's always held the family together. She's stayed behind the scenes, but she's kept everything together."

2. Out of the Shadow

One of the rules of the Hills' home was that Grant couldn't play football until he entered high school. Other sports were fine, but not football. "I didn't want him dealing with the pressure of comparisons," said Calvin. Grant didn't mind at all and instead started to play soccer.

When he was 12, Grant played on a soccer team from Reston that spent a summer playing in tournaments up and down the East Coast. Grant learned to move his feet quickly and developed a skill for darting in different directions with the ball as soon as he received a pass. He was able to transfer some of this dexterity to the basketball court, where he quickly became known for his explosive first steps that allowed him to drive past defenders with ease.

When he was 13, Grant went to St. Louis for a national AAU basketball tournament, where he played against future Michigan University and NBA stars Chris Webber and Jalen Rose. When Calvin watched the warm-ups and saw the quality of top-flight competition Grant had to face, he started preparing a consolation speech for his son.

"I kept looking at those kids, trying to figure out how I was going to scrape Grant off the floor after the game," Calvin recalls. To Calvin's great surprise, however, his son's team won the tournament, and Grant walked away with his first MVP trophy. "After Grant's team won, I gave Chris Webber the same speech I was going to give Grant," Calvin says. "I had no idea how good Grant really was. That was my first glimpse."

While Calvin was bursting with pride, he wanted Grant to learn that every new victory brought new challenges. So when they returned from St. Louis, Calvin had a challenge for Grant. "Bet you still can't beat the old man," said Calvin, who had once scored 59 points in a high school game. Father and son had often played games in the driveway, contests that Calvin had always managed to win. The games had been getting closer, though. And that time, Grant, who had grown to 6-feet-3-inches, finally managed to take Calvin in a game of backyard hoops.

Even more than his MVP performance in the AAU tournament, that game where he finally outscored his father proved to Grant that he really was a good basketball player. However, Grant's ability on the basketball court conflicted with his desire just to blend in with the crowd.

Grant was so concerned about not standing apart from his friends that one time, when he was in the eighth grade and his dad came to give a speech at Langston Hughes Junior High School, Grant pretended to be sick and spent the day in the nurse's office.

Grant never wanted his friends to think that he had a big head because his dad had been a Pro Bowl football player.

Grant was also sensitive about the fact that his parents were financially well off. So one day when Calvin arrived in his Mercedes to pick up his son, Grant asked if, from then on, Calvin would only show up in the family's Volkswagen.

Both Calvin and Grant knew that Grant wasn't going to be able to stand in the shadows forever. That fact became crystal clear one day when Calvin went to the supermarket and realized that he was being trailed by a group of boys. He had been used to that feeling during his days as a pro football player. He was often asked to sign a few autographs and he always willingly obliged. But as Calvin turned to face the boys, expecting to sign his name for them, one of the boys asked, "Hey, aren't you Grant Hill's father?"

Grant was so determined to be just another face in the crowd that he at first refused the opportunity to play for the South Lakes High School varsity basketball team. Grant, who at the time was a ninth-grader, had been looking forward to playing on the junior varsity basketball team alongside the friends he had grown up with. However, Calvin and Wendall Byrd, the South Lakes basketball coach, knew that Grant was ready to skip JV ball and move directly to the varsity. Instead of being thrilled that his ability would allow him to make the big leap, Grant was actually embarrassed that he would, in a basketball sense, be leaving his friends behind him. "You can't make me play," Grant told his stunned father.

Finally, Coach Byrd sat with Grant and rattled off a list of other players' names. "Are you better than so-and-so?" he asked. "What about *him*?" Each time, Grant answered "yes," and reluctantly acknowledged that he probably did deserve to make the varsity team after all.

As soon as Grant signed on, he became the starting point guard at South Lakes. And after moving to forward during tenth grade, he was named Northern Virginia's High School Player of the Year. Still, Grant's growing accomplishments never affected his humble attitude.

When his Dad offered to buy him a Mercedes for his 16th birthday, Grant recalls, "I hated it. I was real sensitive about it. I was like, 'Why can't I have a normal car?'"

Grant may have been willing to settle for an average set of wheels, but on the basketball court, his performance was strictly high octane. He continued his reign as Northern Virginia MVP in his last two seasons at South Lakes, while leading the team into the state finals. In Grant's senior season, he averaged 29 points, 13 rebounds and 7 assists, and was named to the McDonald's High School All-America Team.

Grant also helped the United States win the gold medal at the 1990 Junior World Championships in Uruguay. And he also starred at the McDonald's High School All-Star Game, featuring the finest high school seniors in the nation, including Chris Webber, Jalen Rose and Shawn Bradley, who is currently the starting center for the Philadelphia 76ers.

Grant's basketball skills were simply too impressive for

someone who wanted to blend into the background. Here he was, a 6-feet-7-inch player with superb leaping and ball-handling skills, which allowed him to penetrate like a smaller man and rebound like a bigger man. His quick feet gave him an explosive first step that allowed him to drive past defenders as if their sneakers were nailed to the floor. His knowledge of the game, and his anticipation and work ethic, made him a polished defender who could chase the ball around the court but still cover his man in a post-up situation. Average? No way.

What's more, Grant's enthusiasm for basketball made him a real student of the game. Grant taped NBA games on his VCR and brought his camcorder when he went to see the Georgetown Hoyas play. But instead of dunks and typical highlight-film material, Grant liked to dissect the game's finer points: a perfectly executed pick-and-roll, a backdoor screen or a full-court press. Grant would put the remote on "slow" so he could mimic the players' movements. He rewound and paused tapes so often that he broke five remote controls. Grant picked up this appreciation for detail from Calvin, who understood basketball well and always gave Grant what he called a PGA (short for post-game analysis) after each of his games. After a while, Grant was making his own PGAs.

"Grant taught me things about the game *I* didn't notice," Calvin recalls. "He'd say, 'Hey, check out that backdoor,' and then he'd break it down inch by inch, just like a coach. I swear he knows every move of the 1982 NCAA championship game between Georgetown and North Carolina by heart."

As a special treat for Grant, Calvin took him to see the NCAA Final Four for five straight years between 1984 and 1988. And Calvin also took his grateful son to the 1989 NBA All-Star Game in Houston. Those were fun times for Grant, who never dreamed that *he* would actually *play* in an NBA All-Star or NCAA Final Four game.

3. Off to Duke

Grant was a serious student in the classroom, and he also liked to read in his spare time. His bedroom was filled with school books as well as history books and biographies about Michael Jordan, tennis legend Arthur Ashe, hoop Hall-of-Famers Wilt Chamberlain and Julius Erving, and Georgetown coach John Thompson, all of which Grant read for his own enjoyment.

He especially liked reading about Erving and Ashe, because, as Grant put it, "I could see the kind of people they were off the court as well as on—smart, intelligent, classy people—and admire them for the things they stood for."

In 1990, when it was time for Grant to select a college, he was interested in finding one that had both strong academic standards and a successful basketball program. Initially, he gave the strongest consideration to the two schools that had played in his favorite game: Georgetown and North Carolina.

Grant liked Georgetown for many reasons. It had very strong departments in his areas of interest, history and political science. And for the previous several years, Grant and Calvin had gone to many of the Hoyas' home games at the Capital Centre in Landover, Maryland.

When he went to visit Georgetown, however, Grant was turned off by the treatment he received during a meeting with an academic coordinator. Instead of treating Grant like a serious student, the adviser acted as though Grant was the stereotypical dumb athlete. Grant wanted to be treated as any other student, and he doubted that he would receive that type of treatment at Georgetown.

Grant also had visits planned both to North Carolina and N.C.'s in-state rival, Duke, although Grant considered Duke to be a long shot. But that was before he talked to "Coach K."

Mike Krzyzewski (pronounced sheh-SHEF-ski, but better

known simply as Coach K) was already established as one the most respected coaches in college basketball, having guided the Blue Devils to the NCAA Final Four for the previous three years.

Just as important as the coach's success with building a winning tradition at Duke, Krzyzewski also made sure that the players on his team attended classes and did their schoolwork. Over 90% of the Blue Devil players had graduated since Coach K took over. When the players didn't graduate, Coach K took a strong stand. When, for example, the university had designed a banner for a ceremony commemorating the Blue Devils' trip to the 1990 Final Four, Coach K refused to hang it in Cameron Arena, the team's home court, because three of the squad's seniors had failed to graduate on time.

So it wasn't a big surprise that once Grant made the trip to Raleigh, he would be drawn to Duke based both on the academic programs that were offered and the chance to play for Coach K, especially after the two talked for an hour about Grant's education before they even began to discuss basketball.

In the season opener the following fall against Marquette, Grant became Duke's first freshman starter in six years. Thanks to his versatility, he played all five positions on the court, while Coach K tried to find the best fit for both him and the team. When sophomore point guard Bobby Hurley, who now plays for the Sacramento Kings, picked up his third foul early in the second half, Grant ran the offense and the Blue Devils rolled to victory.

Calvin and Janet went to as many of Grant's games as possible, but Calvin's superstitions kept him away from this one. "He doesn't watch openers," Janet explained when she showed up unaccompanied. "Whenever Grant plays somewhere new, Calvin always skips the first game."

Calvin was always a creature of superstition, but never more so than when he watched Grant play basketball. At Duke games, Calvin developed a routine that was always the same. For every game he wore the same pair of brown loafers, the same khaki slacks, a white shirt (he had several of those) and a Duke hat originally purchased during Grant's recruiting trip and always pulled far down over Calvin's forehead. He always purchased a bag of peanut M&Ms and a pack of Doublemint gum on the way to the arena. Less than one minute before tip-off, he gave precisely three sticks of the gum to Eural (Onion) Lang, the father of Grant's freshman teammate at Duke, Antonio Lang, and hold onto the rest until the second half. In the first half, he always kept the candy in one hand and a cup of ice in the other. In the second half, he'd switch to gum and carry a rolled-up program in both hands. "I have faith in Grant making it through a game okay," joked Janet. "It's Calvin I wonder about."

With Calvin on hand, Duke started the season strong, and so did Grant, who scored in double figures in his first six games as a Blue Devil. "But I was still in awe," he says. "Every game I found myself saying, 'I can't believe I'm playing in (New York's) Madison Square Garden,' or 'I can't believe I'm out on the court with some senior I've watched on TV the last few years.'"

Grant was enjoying his time in college. He had always been the quiet type who liked hanging out with a small group of friends, but campus life helped him open up. He also loved the basketball program at Duke. At times, though, Coach K had to remind Grant not to be as humble on the court as he was off it. "Sometimes it took a little prodding," Krzyzewski said. "We had to tell Grant, 'When you dunk, you're not in the way.'"

4. Yes We Can!

Duke finished the regular season with a record of 26–7. Grant's smart, unselfish play and his smooth gliding moves on the wing were a perfect complement to the Blue Devils' other stars: Hurley, the smallish sophomore point guard who was one of the top playmakers and scorers in the country, and Christian Laettner, the team's flashy junior center and leading scorer, who now plays for the Minnesota Timberwolves.

Duke was one of the top college teams in the country during the 1990–91 season, but no college five seemed capable of upsetting UNLV, the defending NCAA champions, in the 1991 tournament. The powerful Runnin' Rebels had rattled off an undefeated regular season and had won 45 straight games, dating back to the previous season, the fourth longest winning streak in college basketball history.

The Blue Devils did advance to the semifinals for their fourth straight Final Four appearance, but their path to the championship seemed to be absolutely blocked by the high-flying Runnin' Rebels, a powerhouse team fueled by a group of seniors that included Larry Johnson, Stacey Augmon, Greg Anthony and Anderson Hunt, all of whom would be first-round picks in the NBA's 1991 draft.

The UNLV players were very cocky before the game. In a television interview, Augmon began to rattle off his forecast of what would happen on the court: "First two minutes, dunk by Augmon... dunk by Johnson... Ackles over the back dunk... Anthony for three... Anderson Hunt for three... that's it. Duke no score."

Even Krzyzewski spoke about the Runnin' Rebels as though they were unbeatable. "The more tape you watch of them, the more scared you get of them," said Coach K, whose Blue Devils were drubbed by UNLV 103–73 in the 1990 championship game.

"The last time, they beat us by 30, so what are we doing here?"

But an inspired Duke team rallied from a 74–71 deficit and beat UNLV, 79–77. Grant, who played a fine all-around game, was especially tough defensively, holding Augmon, the college Player of the Year, to only six points.

After the final buzzer, the Blue Devils jumped all over each other with joy. Coach K, though, was quick to remind them that they hadn't yet won the national title. "An ordinary team would be satisfied beating UNLV, but an ordinary team won't win on Monday," Krzyzewski said, knowing that Duke still had to beat Kansas two days later to win the big prize.

Grant opened the scoring, as he had done against UNLV. This time, he soared into the air to catch an alley-oop pass and slammed it home for a spectacular one-handed dunk. It was the lead highlight on all the sportscasts that night, and the boy who had grown up reading about his father in *Sports Illustrated* magazine got to see a full two-page spread of his dunk in the same magazine. Grant, who helped the Blue Devils defeat the Jayhawks, 72–65, was also on the magazine's cover with the heading: "Wish Granted. Duke Finally Wins the NCAAs with Help from Freshman Grant Hill."

Although people were starting to look upon Grant as a big-time college star, that status didn't protect him from taking life's little stumbles, such as locking his car keys inside the car at a local car wash, losing the keys to his dormitory room and having his telephone disconnected because he had forgotten to pay one of the bills. "Yeah, he's still 18," said Calvin, one day after Grant forgot to pick him up at the airport. "He's learning how to be responsible just the same as other kids his age."

5. The Greatest Game Ever Played

With all three of Duke's star players—Grant, Hurley and Laettner—due back for the 1991-92 season, the Blue Devils were solid favorites to become the first team in 19 years to repeat as NCAA basketball champions. Duke started living up to the preseason expectations by rolling to a 17–0 record and the number-one spot in the college basketball polls. The team didn't lose a game until February 5, when an ankle sprain kept Grant on the bench and the Blue Devils lost a 75–73 squeaker to the North Carolina Tar Heels. During that game, Hurley also went down with what seemed to be a mild foot injury. The next day, Grant walked into class, and a friend whispered in his ear, "Did you know that Bobby's in a cast?"

Grant thought the classmate was kidding, but it turned out to be true. Without Hurley, the team's top play maker, Grant would have to move from his forward position back into Hurley's point guard spot, where he would take over as the team's floor general.

It was not a role that Grant would have chosen for himself. "I'm not a leader. I don't want to be in that situation," the player who was nicknamed the Reluctant Superstar admitted to Hurley. Aware of Grant's feelings about himself, Coach K pulled Grant aside and told him, "Don't be afraid to be good. You can be a tremendous threat on offense if you assert yourself and be more creative."

It was a sort of catch-22 for Grant, who always felt that if he took over a leadership role he would be thrusting himself into the limelight. Yet his parents had brought him up to be humble and not to puff himself up. That upbringing often made Grant reluctant to step forward and take charge.

Grant, though, responded positively to the challenge and ran Coach K's offense until Hurley was able to return. The Blue

Devils finished the regular season at 28–2, and their confidence was soaring. "There was this air that we had during the season," Grant recalls. "Our whole approach was, 'Hey, what team even has the *audacity* to be on the court with us?'"

But one team, the Kentucky Wildcats, took up the challenge in a big way on a March afternoon in Philadelphia, at the regional final of the NCAA tournament. The Wildcats, led by Jamal Mashburn who would go on to NBA stardom with the Dallas Mavericks, were audacious enough to give the Blue Devils a fight for their lives in what many consider the greatest college basketball game ever played.

For a while it seemed neither side could miss. During one sequence, the teams made 13 straight shots: running jumpers, bank shots, three-pointers. Everything was falling.

Although Duke managed to build a ten-point lead, the Wildcats fought back and forced the game into overtime when Hurley missed a last-second shot. "I couldn't believe it was going into overtime," Grant recalled later. "It was the toughest 40 minutes of basketball I'd ever played, and it was just getting started."

With 2.1 seconds left in O.T., the game seemed all but finished when Kentucky's Sean Woods banked in a shot that gave the Wildcats a one-point lead. During a time-out that Duke called immediately after Woods' basket, Coach K outlined a desperation play that called for Grant to throw a football-like pass from one end of the court all the way to the opposite foul circle, where Laettner would be expected to snatch the pass and put up a buzzer-beating shot.

The pass had to be pin-point perfect, giving Laettner a chance to catch, turn and shoot. Duke's senior center had played the game of his life until that point, scoring 29 points without missing a shot from anywhere: 9-of-9 from the floor (including one three-pointer) and 10-of-10 from the foul line.

Placed in a do-or-die situation, Grant tossed a perfect one-handed court-length pass towards Laettner. While the ball was still in the air, Laettner rolled away from a pick, snared the ball, faked and let the shot go just before the buzzer sounded.

Swish!

Laettner flung his fists over his head and Grant leaped in the air, as the Duke team and its fans exploded with joy at their 104–103 victory. On the opposite side of the arena, Calvin and Janet Hill were wondering if the stands were going to withstand the pounding of jumping feet. "If they collapse and I die, I'm going to die happy," Calvin screamed.

What made the game rank among the all-time top collegiate contests wasn't merely the fact that it all came down to a last-second buzzer-beating bucket in overtime, or even that it happened during a tension-filled NCAA regional final. What helped to elevate this game to the level of greatness was the outstanding shooting display by both teams. Duke had set a school record for field-goal percentage, making 34 of 52 shots for 65%. Kentucky, meanwhile, clicked on 37 of 65 shots, including 12 of 22 three-pointers, for a sizzling 57% from downtown.

Afterwards, reporters jokingly asked Grant if he might consider trying out for professional football after all—as a quarterback. "No, there will only be one game like that and I can only throw one pass like that," said Grant, who finished with 11 points, 10 rebounds and 7 assists, and his modesty intact.

Kentucky Coach Rick Pitino put the game in perspective when he told the Wildcats, "You've been a part of something glorious. You may be crying now, but hold your heads up, because this is not the game of life; it's the game of basketball, and today you played it about as well as a team ever has without winning."

Coach K could hardly believe it. "I really am stunned. Did that just happen?" he asked. "I think we've just been a part of history."

6. Repeat

The Blue Devils didn't have the luxury of relaxing after their emotionally draining victory against the Wildcats. They still had to win two more games in order to repeat as national champions, and Coach K made sure his team didn't forget that a match-up against a tough Indiana team awaited them.

"We're not the greatest thing since sliced bread, you know," he told the squad during practice. "If we play tomorrow the way we look today, Indiana will wipe us all over the court."

Despite Coach K's pep talk, Duke trailed Indiana by five at half-time. Throughout the first half, the Hoosiers had executed a strong game plan by denying entry passes to Laettner, who made only one of six shots during the first 20 minutes.

The Blue Devils had their backs to the wall and needed Grant's versatility to help bail them out of trouble. For much of the second half, Coach K asked some of his players to swap positions in order to confuse Indiana's defense. Grant moved to the point guard spot, so he could find open shots for Hurley. Playing the unfamiliar role of shooting guard, Bobby stepped up and led all scorers with 26 points. With nine minutes to play in the second half, the Blue Devils had forged an amazing 25-point turnaround and built a 60–47 lead. Although the Hoosiers finally adjusted and battled back, Duke held on for an 81–78 victory.

After squeaking by against an experienced Indiana squad, the Blue Devils were set to face Michigan in the final. The Wolverines were the youngest team in NCAA tournament history, sporting a starting line-up of freshmen known as "The Fab Five." The group included Chris Webber and Jalen Rose, whom Grant had faced years earlier in the AAU tournament, as well as Juwon Howard, who now plays with Webber on the Washington Bullets. If the Blue Devils could control the fast-breaking, board-crashing Wolverines, they would become the first team to win back-to-back NCAA titles since UCLA in 1973, the year Michigan's Fab Five were all born.

Yet, surprisingly, it was the veteran Duke team that played without poise in the first half. Michigan led 31–30 at halftime, and the struggling Laettner had seven turnovers, and just two points and a pair of rebounds. Coach K, who is usually mild-mannered, was so angry that he smashed a blackboard in the locker room. "Forget the Kentucky game, already! It's not our *destiny* to win," the coach said. "It's our *choice*. We have to *work* for it."

In the second half, Grant responded to Coach K's remarks by breaking open the close game with three straight baskets. Each time, he had a different Wolverine trying to guard him. His work on the wing also opened up the middle for Hurley's penetration and Laettner's shooting. After taking a 48–45 lead, the Blue Devils went on a decisive 10–2 run that ended when Grant flew along the base line and threw down a dunk that gave Duke its first double-digit lead of the game. He also blocked a shot and grabbed three rebounds in that stretch, as the Blue Devils scored on 12 of 13 possessions, while holding the Wolverines to 20 second-half points in a convincing 71–51 victory.

"Grant was the key to the game," Coach K said later. "He woke the rest of us up."

In the game, Grant pumped in 18 points and hauled down 10 rebounds. As usual, Grant's good play helped contribute to the success of others. During the tournament, Laettner set the all-time career record for tournament points with 407, breaking the former mark of 359 that had been established by Elvin Hayes in 1968. Hurley also passed Sherman Douglas for first place on the all-time tournament assist list with his 107th. When both Hurley and Laettner were asked about their accomplishments, they both mentioned the fact that Grant's unselfish play contributed to the team's success.

"He posts good numbers. They just happen to be *our*

numbers," Bobby said, explaining that Grant did all the little things that sometimes didn't show up in boxscores but that often provided the foundation for a championship team.

7. Humble Pie

While Grant was learning to become a leader on the court, he was also becoming an articulate spokesman for the values in which he believed. He appeared with the Duke's president on the Charlie Rose show, a highly respected PBS talk show, where both men talked about the importance of education. Grant had applied himself so well that he was able to quote the Greek philosopher Aristotle during a speech at the National Association of Basketball Coaches Issues Forum.

Grant was also a model student in other ways. He was too modest to wear his championship rings around campus and too smart to sample alcohol, a substance that he still avoids. When Grant speaks to younger students, especially those in high school, he tells them, "The percentages of making it as a professional athlete are far less than making it as a doctor or lawyer. One day you have to put the baseball or the basketball down. But what you learned upstairs in your head will stay with you for the rest of your life."

During his third season at Duke, Grant found out just how precarious an athletic career can be when he broke his big toe on February 13. The injury temporarily limited his movement, and left him unable to use that explosive first step that he had relied on to score most of his points. "We don't want people trying to take Grant's place," Coach K said. "Not everybody can do what Grant does."

Grant also found out how fleeting fame can be and how champions can lose their crown, when the Blue Devils were stunned by the University of California in the second game of the NCAA tournament, 82–77. Cal's point guard Jason Kidd, who has gone on to become a star play maker for the Dallas Mavericks, was too much for the Blue Devils' defense to handle, and after 13 straight postseason victories, Grant had tasted his first NCAA tournament loss.

After the season, Grant was voted the nation's best defensive player, but his broken toe hadn't healed properly, and he had to undergo off-season surgery, which kept him off the court from April until August.

But win or lose, injured or healthy, Grant never seemed to lose his easy-going cool. "I was emotionally explosive as an athlete, and you always know how Janet feels, but Grant amazes me sometimes," Calvin said. "He never changes his expression. I often wonder what's going on inside. There must be a lot bubbling, a lot that gets channeled."

8. The Duke of Duke

With both Laettner and Hurley playing in the NBA, the 1993-94 season was supposed to have been a rebuilding year for the Blue Devils, just the kind of season that would make life difficult for Grant, their new senior captain, whom fans were now calling "The Duke of Duke." Captains, after all, were not expected to blend into the background.

"Once Grant was actually asked to be in the spotlight, once he understood that it was his responsibility to assume the attention, he didn't mind at all," said Tommy Amaker, one of Coach K's assistant coaches.

At Krzyzewski's urging, Grant was shooting three-pointers with regularity. In Grant's first two years, he had attempted only three shots from downtown, sinking one. In his junior year, he made 4 of 14. But as a senior, Grant improved to 39-of-100. What's more, Grant began to take a more vocal role in team huddles, patting teammates on the back, speaking up when needed, and leading the celebrations for his teammates after they made an especially nice play.

Shortly after the midseason mark, Grant took freshman Jeff Capel aside for the type of pep talk he, himself, had received from older teammates a few years earlier. Capel later said he felt a new level of confidence after his talk with Grant. "He's one of the reasons I chose to come here," Capel said after the game. "I always wanted to have a chance to play with him."

Afterwards, Coach K marveled, "We're 17–3 in what many people thought would be a rebuilding year. The main reason for that is Grant."

The team finished with a 22–4 regular season mark, but lost some momentum heading into the NCAA tournament after losing badly to Virginia in the ACC conference quarter-finals.

The Blue Devils got back on track by bouncing Texas Southern in their opening tournament game. But then they had to take on Michigan State, which featured hot-shooting guard Shawn Respert, who had been averaging 24.4 points-per-game. However, thanks to Grant's stifling defense, Respert was only able to get off one shot in the first half and didn't get on the scoreboard until midway through the second half.

Grant, who held Respert to 10 points, scored 25 points, handed out 7 assists and made 4 steals as Duke emerged with an 85–74 victory. "Every time I made a move," said Respert, who was a first round pick in the 1995 NBA draft, "Grant was there. Even when you think you've lost him, he gets right into your face. He's got to be the quickest player on earth."

Nevertheless, even though Grant had become more assertive in his role as team captain, he still had difficulty in trying to claim a starring role for himself. In Duke's next game against Marquette, for example, the Blue Devils found themselves down by a basket one minute into the second half. But during a time out, instead of asking Coach K to run plays for him, Grant calmly remarked to a couple of his teammates that he was feeling good about his shot. Krzyzewski heard the remark and called the next three plays for Grant, who made two shots and drew a loose-ball foul on those three possessions. "He was too embarrassed to say anything directly to me," Coach K said later. "But I got his message."

Grant wound up shooting 10-of-16 for a team-high 22 points against a Marquette team that had led the nation in field-goal defense, while pacing Duke to a 59–49 victory.

Duke's next game, a regional final against the 29–4 Purdue Boilermakers, provided college basketball fans with a marquee match-up between two of college basketball's top two players, Grant and Glenn Robinson. If Duke hoped to advance to the Final Four, Grant would have to put a muzzle on "Big Dog" Robinson, who was averaging nearly 31 points per game and was generally regarded to be the college player of the year. The game was being billed as a struggle between Robinson, college basketball's most lethal scorer, and Grant, who had just won his second consecutive Henry Iba Award as college basketball's outstanding defensive player.

The expected showdown turned into a no-contest, though, as Grant clamped down on Big Dog, holding him to 13 points, his lowest scoring game of the season, and sparked Duke to a 69–60 victory.

The Blue Devils then traveled to Charlotte, North Carolina, not far from their home arena in Durham, for a Final Four meeting against Florida. Duke struggled early and trailed by as many as 13 points, but Grant keyed the team's come-from-behind victory by playing all 40 minutes, scoring 25 points, and adding six rebounds and five assists.

After the game, Krzyzewski declared, "Grant is the best player I've coached. Christian Laettner told me that when he was a senior, and Bobby Hurley said the same thing, so I don't think I'm hurting any feelings. We've been lucky to have him for the ride, and I have to admit, I didn't expect to get this far this year."

Grant's college basketball career ended on a sour note, though, as Duke lost to Arkansas in the final, 76–72. Grant scored 12 points and hauled down 14 rebounds, but the Razorbacks pulled out the game in the final minute. President Clinton, formerly the governor of Arkansas, led the cheers for his Razorbacks, but confessed later, "That was one tough 'Hill' to climb."

Grant's all-around skills were highlighted by the fact that he became the first player in ACC history to record at least 1900 (1924) points, 700 (769) rebounds, 400 (461) assists, 200 (218) steals and 100 (133) blocked shots. More important than even that singular achievement, Grant had used his unique talents to help Duke compile a 117–22 record and reach the Final Four three times in four seasons at Duke. In a tribute both to his own skills and his contributions to the team's success, the Duke athletic department decided to raise his number 33 to the rafters of Cameron Arena, making Grant only the eighth basketball player in Duke history to have his number retired.

But perhaps most important, Grant was able to honor himself, his parents and the university when he marched into Wallace Wade Stadium in his cap and gown, having graduated on time with a degree both in history and political science.

9. Motown Bound

Because of their poor record during the 1993-94 season, the Detroit Pistons had drawn the third pick in the NBA's draft lottery and felt they had a shot at drafting Grant, the college player who was at the top of their wish list. It wasn't only his playing ability that they liked; the team also needed a young star with maturity and a stable personality, a player whom they could build a team around.

For several years, the Pistons had cultivated an image: the Bad Boys of Motown. The Detroit teams of the late 1980s were scrappy, physical and mean. But they were also just plain good. The Pistons reached the finals for three straight years and won NBA titles in 1989 and 1990, before they were dethroned by Michael Jordan and the Chicago Bulls.

But the Detroit organization was so determined to change the image of the Pistons that it had almost entirely transformed the team, retaining only Joe Dumars, the veteran shooting guard.

Dumars's easy-going, gentlemanly personality was a sharp contrast to most of the troubled team that had fizzled into an embarrassment both to its ownership and its fans. The Pistons wanted Dumars to pass the torch on to a player the franchise could be proud of, on and off the court.

Tom Wilson, the team president, and Billy McKinney, the Vice President of Basketball Operations, were at the Pistons' draft headquarters in Detroit, waiting for the Milwaukee Bucks and Dallas Mavericks to announce their picks. Rumors suggested that the Bucks would take Purdue's Glenn Robinson with the first pick and that the Mavericks, who already had Jamal Mashburn aa small forward and were in desperate need of a point guard, would take Cal's Jason Kidd with the second, leaving Detroit with a chance to select Grant, the player they desperately wanted.

Milwaukee did choose Robinson, but the Pistons still had to sweat out the Mavs' pick. McKinney was a nervous wreck. "I was breathing erratically and I literally held my breath when the Mavericks were making their pick," said McKinney, who began crying when he heard the announcement. "When I finally heard Kidd's name, I thought to myself, 'Finally, something went right for this team.'"

After the draft, the Pistons began negotiations to try to sign Grant as quickly as possible. At the same time that other players were skipping training camp in order to hold out for larger contracts, Grant and his parents had already used some money from an agreement with an apparel sponsor to make a contribution to an inner-city basketball program in the Motor City area. Grant also asked Pistons' assistant coach Brendan Malone for tapes from the team's championship years so that he could study Detroit's offensive and defensive plays.

Grant's eagerness to do good deeds and to fit in with the Detroit organization thrilled members of the Pistons' management. "As good a player as Grant Hill is, I actually think he's a better person. He spoke so well, listened well, and knew so much about the history of our organization," said McKinney. "It was like he studied up on us."

The Pistons quickly signed Grant to an eight-year, $45-million contract. It was a sign of the times that he would make more money in his rookie year than his father had made in his entire NFL career.

Before training camp at the team's home arena in Auburn Hills, Michigan, Dumars, the Pistons' captain, asked if the team would assign Grant a locker next to his. More than any other member of the Pistons' championship team, Dumars had developed a reputation as a quiet leader. When asked what he liked about Grant, Don Chaney, the Pistons' coach at the time, responded, "When I think of Grant Hill, I think of Joe Dumars, and that's the highest compliment I could ever pay the young man."

As hoped, the rookie and the veteran became fast friends. Every day during practice, Grant would ask Joe a bunch of questions. "I feel like I'm a sponge," Grant said. "I'm soaking up everything, and Joe's gone out of his way to make me feel a part of the team."

Dumars was just as complimentary. "I've never seen a player so young who just never gets rattled by anything," he said. "He has a lot of confidence that he doesn't want to flaunt in front of everybody's face the way some people do. I feel privileged to play with him for the next three or four years."

Grant started off his pro career on a high note. In his first NBA contest, he picked up a loose ball and drove for a dunk five seconds after he entered the game.

Detroit surprisingly won five of its first seven games and Grant—no great surprise—was named the NBA Rookie of the Month for November. Grant's dynamic play in the open floor and his ability to create shots for both himself and his teammates drew instant comparisons with the NBA's elite players.

Boston's Dominique Wilkins, who has scored over 25,000 points in his 13-year NBA career, was instantly impressed with Grant the first time the Celtics faced the Pistons. "He gets to the hole the way I did when I first came up," said Wilkins, a one-time NBA scoring champion and slam-dunk contest winner. "But with him, it's not just quick; it's really well thought out, like he just goes so you can't reach him."

Other NBA players, such as Alonzo Mourning, the All-Star center of the Charlotte Hornets, also marveled at the rookie's skills. "Grant is the key to the Pistons' future," Mourning said. "The sky is the limit for him."

As Grant traveled around the league, a lot of people even started to compare him to Michael Jordan, the Chicago Bulls' superstar who retired for a year and a half before coming back near the end of the 1994-95 season. Both players coincidentally had won national championships with ACC teams (Jordan won his at North Carolina) and both were picked third in the NBA draft (Jordan in 1984). Both players loved running in the open floor and seemed to be able to float in the air while scoring over defenders. Both players also spent time during their careers at point guard, even though Jordan is primarily a shooting guard and Grant is most often used as small forward.

But it was the similarity in their styles of play that caught people's attention. The ability to accelerate past a defender and float to the basket caused those people to think that Grant could be a Jordan in the making. When, for example, a television sportscaster asked Dumars what made Grant so special, Dumars said, "He simply explodes to the basket. And that *control*. Once he gets by a guy, he is so in control. The first time I played him in a scrimmage, his first move was just—boom!—right on by me. And there is only one guy I've seen do that."

"Joe, do you mean..."

"Yes I do."

However, there were other, perhaps, keener observers, including Coach Chaney, who thought the comparisons weren't fair to either player.

"Right now, people are putting him on a level with Michael, and it concerns me," Coach Chaney told reporters. "You're asking a rookie to live up to a reputation he hasn't even attained yet. Hill will be a great player, but the fun's in the journey. Let's not rush him."

Larry Brown, the veteran coach of the Indiana Pacers, put the discussion in a useful perspective. "He can't get caught up in whether he's going to be the next Michael, because there is never going to be another Michael," said Brown. "But then, I don't know if there is ever going to be another Grant Hill. If he continues to develop, there are going to be a lot of young kids out there who'll want to be just like him. You know what, that's exactly what our game needs."

Despite Grant's fast start, opposing teams soon exploited the

Pistons' inexperience. For Grant, who had lost only 22 games during his entire four years at Duke, it was hard to watch the team lose its 22nd game by midseason and harder still when a foot injury kept him out of action for 12 games during the team's December slump.

In some other ways, life hadn't changed much for Grant. He still ate shrimp fried rice several days a week, drank Cherry Kool-Aid, watched his favorite Eddie Murphy movies, played video games and hung out at the local Barnes & Noble bookstore, where he'd sit and read for hours. He also regularly played the piano as a way to relax and clear his mind.

Although some things were the same in Detroit, Grant was still having some difficulty adjusting to his new environment. He not only missed winning, he also missed his friends at school, the challenging, but relaxed atmosphere of the class-room, and the days he could play some ping-pong and joke around with people he had known for four years. "Enjoy your last few months before graduation," he'd told his friends who were still at Duke. "I thought I'd be glad to get on with my life, but college really is the best time. Enjoy it."

10. All-Star

Grant's behavior made him the sort of person people wanted to look up to, and he did not shy away from being put on that sort of pedestal. "I live my life as if I'm running for president," he once said. "Some people think athletes shouldn't be role models, but we *are* role models, whether we like it or not. Personally, I welcome the responsibility."

One night while walking to a friend's house in Detroit with teammates Johnny Dawkins and Raphael Addison, Grant stopped to talk to a homeless man who had asked them for money. His teammates looked on, unsure of just what to say. "Grant is a very humble person," Addison said later. "All day he was talking about that guy. Most of us would have passed him by, not given it a second thought."

Those around him appreciated the way that Grant treated other people. "You have to give credit to the program he came from and also his parents," Coach Chaney said. "He can deal with a lot of different situations. He's so popular. He's able to accommodate reporters and fans, and yet still stay focused on basketball."

Fans liked him so much, they did something unprecedented for a rookie. They not only chose him to represent the Eastern Conference at the NBA All-Star Game in Phoenix, they voted for him more often than any player in the league. No other rookie in the history of the NBA had ever finished first in the fans' voting. Grant received 1,289,585 votes, roughly 26,000 ahead of Orlando's Shaquille O'Neal, the East's starting center. One Seattle writer said her ideal game would be "an All-Star game played solely by Grant Hills. Five Grant Hill starters for the East, five for the West and about a dozen more on the benches."

Still, Grant couldn't believe that he was being placed in such elite company. "It's a little embarrassing, actually. I'm a rookie. I don't think I deserve to be an All-Star," said Grant, who, despite

89

his fine all-around play, was not in the top-ten in any statistical category. But over the previous few years, NBA players had slowly been gaining a reputation for whining and complaining as much as playing. *Sports Illustrated* even ran a cover story entitled "Whah" about the fact that certain players were giving the league a bad name because of their "trash talking" and boorish behavior. Grant's popularity was not only a compliment to his playing ability and his pleasant personality, but also a statement that fans cared about the way players conducted themselves. It was simple: Calvin hadn't spiked the ball after touchdowns, and Grant wouldn't talk trash after dunks.

Both Hill and Dumars represented the Pistons in the All-Star Game, which was Joe's fifth appearance in the midseason classic. Late in the first half, his backcourt teammate set up Grant for three straight baskets, including a highlight-film, alley-oop dunk. Grant played 20 minutes and finished with ten points. He committed only one turnover, but missed all four of his free-throw attempts and confessed to a bad case of the jitters. "I was so nervous being on the floor with those guys, I was almost sick to my stomach a few times," Grant said. "When they introduced us to pregame fireworks, I thought somebody was trying to shoot me."

After playing in the All-Star Game, Grant found that going back to play with Detroit was tough. Grant had never played on a team that had lost more than it had won. "How do you adjust to losing?" asked Grant, whose fine play wasn't enough to stop the Pistons from finishing with a 28–54 record. "I can't adjust. It hurts the same way it hurt in college, when we hardly *ever lost*."

Grant ended the season as one of the few bright spots on an otherwise dull team. He led the Pistons with a 19.9 points-per-game average, and added 6.4 rebounds and 5.0 assists per game. Grant's numbers and sound all-around play were enough to earn him co-Rookie-of-the-Year honors along with Dallas' Jason Kidd, but they weren't enough to satisfy him. When asked how he planned to celebrate his outstanding first year during the off-season, Grant answered, "By working on my game. I have a lot of work to do. Our team has work to do."

Instead of looking back at what he had accomplished, Grant was acting like a true champion, looking forward to new challenges for himself and his team.

Sources

The Associated Press

The Boston Globe

The Chicago Sun Times

The Chicago Tribune

The Commercial Appeal

The Detroit Free Press

Duke University Athletic Department

ESPN

The Indianapolis Star

The Los Angeles Times

Memphis State University Athletic Department

National Basketball Association

The New York Times

The Orlando Sentinel

People Magazine

The Sporting News

Sports Illustrated

Sports Illustrated for Kids

USA Today

The Washington Post

ANFERNEE DEON HARDAWAY

Birthdate: July 18, 1971

Birthplace: Memphis, Tennessee

Height: 6 ft., 7 in.

Weight: 200 lbs.

MEMPHIS STATE UNIVERSITY STATS

YEAR	G/GS	FG/A	PCT	FT/A	PCT	REB	AVG	PF/D	AST	TO	BLK	STL	PTS	AVG
1991-92	34/34	209/483	.433	103/158	.652	237	7.0	92/4	188	125	45	86	590	17.4
1992-93	32/32	249/522	.477	158/206	.767	273	8.5	86/2	204	109	39	76	729	22.8
TOTALS	66/66	458/1005	.456	261/364	.717	510	7.7	178/6	392	234	84	162	1319	20.0

NBA REGULAR SEASON STATS

YEAR/TEAM	G	MIN	FGM	FGA	PCT	FTM	FTA	PCT	OFF	DEF	TOT	AST	PF	DQ	STL	BLK	PTS	AVG
1993-94 Orl	82	3015	509	1092	.466	245	330	.742	192	247	439	544	205	2	190	51	1313	16.0
1994-95 Orl	77	2901	585	1142	.512	356	463	.769	139	197	336	551	158	1	130	26	1613	20.9
TOTALS	159	5916	1094	2234	.490	601	793	.768	331	444	775	1095	363	3	320	77	2926	18.4

NBA PLAYOFF STATS

YEAR/TEAM	G	MIN	FGM	FGA	PCT	FTM	FTA	PCT	OFF	DEF	TOT	AST	PF	DQ	STL	BLK	PTS	AVG
1993-94 Orl	3	133	22	50	.440	7	10	.700	8	12	20	21	10	0	5	6	56	18.7
1994-95 Orl	21	849	144	305	.472	84	111	.757	30	49	79	162	70	0	40	15	412	19.6
TOTALS	24	982	166	355	.468	91	121	.752	38	61	99	183	80	0	45	21	468	19.5

GRANT HENRY HILL
Birthdate: October 5, 1972
Birthplace: Dallas, Texas
Height: 6 ft., 8 in.
Weight: 225 lbs.

DUKE UNIVERSITY STATS

YEAR	G/GS	FG/A	PCT	FT/A	PCT	REB	AVG	AST	BLK	STL	PTS	AVG
1990-91	36/31	160/310	.516	81/133	.609	183	5.1	79	30	51	402	11.2
1991-92	33/24	182/298	.611	99/135	.733	187	5.7	134	27	39	463	14.0
1992-93	26/26	185/320	.578	94/126	.746	166	6.4	72	36	64	468	18.0
1993-94	34/34	218/472	.462	116/165	.703	233	6.9	176	40	64	591	17.4
TOTALS	129/115	745/1400	.532	390/559	.698	769	6.0	461	133	218	1924	14.9

NBA REGULAR SEASON STATS

YEAR/TEAM	G	MIN	FGM	FGA	PCT	FTM	FTA	PCT	OFF	DEF	TOT	AST	PF	DQ	STL	BLK	PTS	AVG
1993-94 Det	70	2678	508	1064	.477	374	511	.732	125	320	445	353	203	1	124	62	1394	19.9

If you enjoyed this book, you might want to order some of our other exciting titles:

BASKETBALL SUPERSTARS ALBUM 1996, Richard J. Brenner. Includes 16 full-color pages, and mini-bios of the game's top superstars, plus career and all-time stats. 48 pages.

MICHAEL JORDAN * MAGIC JOHNSON, by Richard J. Brenner. A dual biography of two of the greatest superstars of all time. 128 pages, 15 dynamite photos.

ANFERNEE HARDAWAY * GRANT HILL, by Brian Cazeneuve. A dual biography of two of the brightest young stars in basketball. 96 pages, 10 pages of photos.

SHAQUILLE O'NEAL * LARRY JOHNSON, by Richard J. Brenner. A dual biography of two of the brightest young stars in basketball. 96 pages, 10 pages of photos.

STEVE YOUNG * JERRY RICE, by Richard J. Brenner. A dual biography of the two superstars who led the 49ers to the Super Bowl. 96 pages, 10 pages of photos.

TROY AIKMAN * STEVE YOUNG, by Richard J. Brenner. A dual biography of the top two quarterbacks in the NFL. 96 pages, 10 pages of photos.

KEN GRIFFEY JR. * FRANK THOMAS, by Brian Cazeneuve. A dual biography of two of baseball's brightest young superstars. 96 pages, 10 pages of photos.

BARRY BONDS * ROBERTO ALOMAR, by Bob Woods. A dual biography of two of the brightest stars in baseball. 96 pages, 10 pages of photos.

MARIO LEMIEUX, by Richard J. Brenner. An exciting biography of one of hockey's all-time greats. 96 pages, 10 pages of photos.

THE WORLD SERIES, THE GREAT CONTESTS, by Richard J. Brenner. The special excitement of the Fall Classic is brought to life through seven of the most thrilling Series ever played, including 1993. 176 pages, including 16 action-packed photos.

THE COMPLETE SUPER BOWL STORY, GAMES I-XXVIII, by Richard J. Brenner. The most spectacular moments in Super Bowl history are brought to life, game by game. 224 pages, including 16 memorable photos.

MICHAEL JORDAN, by Richard J. Brenner. An easy-to-read, photo-filled biography especially for younger readers. 32 pages.

SHAQUILLE O'NEAL, by Richard J. Brenner. An easy-to-read, photo-filled biography especially for younger readers. 32 pages.

WAYNE GRETZKY, by Richard J. Brenner. An easy-to-read, photo-filled biography especially for younger readers. 32 pages.

TOUCHDOWN! THE FOOTBALL FUN BOOK, by Richard J. Brenner. Trivia, puzzles, mazes and much more! 64 pages.

PLEASE SEE NEXT PAGE FOR ORDER FORM

ORDER FORM

Payment must accompany all orders and must be in U.S. dollars.
Postage and handling is $1.35 per book up to a maximum of $6.75 ($1.75 to a maximum of $8.75 in Canada).

Please send me the following books:

No. of copies	Title	Price
_____	BASKETBALL SUPERSTARS ALBUM 1996	$4.50/$6.25 Can.
_____	MICHAEL JORDAN * MAGIC JOHNSON	$3.50/$4.25 Can.
_____	ANFERNEE HARDAWAY * GRANT HILL	$3.99/$5.50 Can.
_____	SHAQUILLE O'NEAL * LARRY JOHNSON	$3.50/$4.50 Can.
_____	STEVE YOUNG * JERRY RICE	$3.99/$5.50 Can.
_____	TROY AIKMAN * STEVE YOUNG	$3.50/$4.50 Can.
_____	KEN GRIFFEY JR. * FRANK THOMAS	$3.50/$4.50 Can.
_____	BARRY BONDS * ROBERTO ALOMAR	$3.50/$4.50 Can.
_____	MARIO LEMIEUX	$3.50/$4.50 Can.
_____	THE WORLD SERIES, THE GREAT CONTESTS	$3.50/$4.50 Can.
_____	THE COMPLETE SUPER BOWL STORY GAMES I-XXVIII	$4.00/$5.00 Can.
_____	MICHAEL JORDAN	$4.00/$5.50 Can.
_____	SHAQUILLE O'NEAL	$3.25/$4.50 Can.
_____	WAYNE GRETZKY	$3.25/$4.50 Can.
_____	TOUCHDOWN! THE FOOTBALL FUN BOOK	$3.50/$5.00 Can.

TOTAL NUMBER OF BOOKS ORDERED _____

TOTAL PRICE OF BOOKS $_____

POSTAGE AND HANDLING $_____

TOTAL PAYMENT ENCLOSED $_____

NAME _____

ADDRESS _____

CITY _____ STATE _____ ZIP _____ COUNTRY _____

Send to: East End Publishing, 54 Alexander Drive, Syosset NY 11791 USA. Dept. TD. Allow three weeks for delivery. Discounts are available on orders of 25 or more copies. For details call (516) 364-6383.